Phonetic Storybook 11

ow • ou • ōw • ew • wh • silent l

PEARSON

Longman

Contents

Raceway Step 24A
Words with **ow, ou**

Cody the Clown Comes to Town   3
By Vida Daly

A Brownie Scout   20
By Sue Dickson

Raceway Step 24B
Words with **ōw, ew**

The Snowman   31
By Hetty Hubbard

The New Crew   39
By Lynda MacDonald and Sue Dickson

Raceway Step 24C
Words with **qu, wh**

Quite a Surprise   47
By Hetty Hubbard

The New White Car   54
By Hetty Hubbard

2

Cody the Clown Comes to Town

By Vida Daly

Illustrations by Laurence Cleyet-Merle

Vocabulary Words

1. bow	12. Howard
2. bowed	13. howl
3. brown	14. howled
4. chow	15. now
5. clown	16. owl
6. clowns	17. shower
7. cow	18. towel
8. down	19. town
9. flower	20. Wow
10. frown	**Story Words**
11. gown	bath tub
	21. bathtub

22. circus

23. Cody

24. dressed

25. finished

26. Hi

27. Molly

28. Molly's

29. painted

30. rushed

31. Sandy

32. skinny

33. taking

34. upside

Molly jumped from her bed and ran to take a shower. Then, she dried off with her green towel and ran to get dressed.

Today was Molly's big day. The circus had come to town at last!

"Hurry down to eat," yelled Mom. "It's nine o'clock now. We must be in town by ten. I will feed Sandy some dog chow. Then, we will go. Uncle Howard will meet us at the big tent."

When Molly finished eating, she asked, "May we go now? I can't wait to see the circus!"

"Yes, it is time to go now," said Mom.

Uncle Howard met Mom and Molly at the big tent.

Molly looked way up to the top. "Wow!" cried Molly.

"It is big," said Uncle Howard.

"Now, come with me, Molly. We will go see Cody the Clown," said Uncle Howard.

Uncle Howard and Cody were pals.

"Hi, Molly," said Cody. "Would you like to see me paint my face?"

"Wow! Yes!" said Molly.

Cody the Clown put
thick white cream on
his face.

Then, he painted fat red
lips. Next, he put a big
pink spot on each cheek.

"Now, what is missing?"
asked Cody with a frown.

"Your big red nose!"
said Molly.

Cody put on his huge
red nose and bowed to
Molly. Molly just howled!

Then, Cody, Uncle Howard, Mom, and Molly rushed to the big tent.

"I must not miss my big act," said Cody. "I will wave to you, Molly. Have fun at the circus today."

Molly liked all the
clowns . . . fat clowns,
skinny clowns, red clowns,
and brown clowns.

One clown was in a
funny gown, upside down!
A second clown was in
a bathtub taking a shower!

There was a clown with a brown owl and a clown with a flower.

There was a clown that could howl and a clown with a brown cow.

Best of all, there was
Cody taking a bow!

The End

A Brownie Scout

by Sue Dickson

Illustrations by Marsha Winborn

Vocabulary Words

1. around
2. couch
3. flour
4. found
5. ground
6. hour
7. house
8. loud
9. our
10. Proud
11. Scout
12. Scouting
13. Scouts
14. shout
15. shouted
sound
16. sounds

Story Words

17. Brownie
18. camp-out
19. Kara
20. Kara's
21. leader
22. lives
(Mis iz)
23. Mrs.
24. oven
25. paper
(sez)
26. says

Kara ran into the house. "Mom!" she shouted. "Look at this paper. Our teacher gave it to us. It says that Pam's mom is the Brownie Scout leader. May I be a Brownie Scout?" she asked.

"That sounds like fun," said Kara's mom. "Maybe we could ask Mrs. Proud to tell us what Brownie Scouts is all about."

"Pam and Mrs. Proud live just around the block," said Kara. "May we go see them now?"

Mom said, "I need to finish this pie and wipe the flour off my hands. Then, we will see."

24

When Mom had finished,
she spoke to Mrs. Proud.
"Mrs. Proud has time to
see us," she said to Kara.

So Kara and her mom
went to visit Mrs. Proud
and Pam.

"We would like to find out about Brownie Scouts," said Kara.

Mrs. Proud said, "Please come in. You can sit here on our couch."

Mrs. Proud began to tell Mom and Kara about scouting. She said, "Our Brownie Scouts will go on a camp-out. We will sleep on the ground in tents. Do you have a sleeping bag, Kara?"

"Yes, " said Kara.
"Daddy has a sleeping
bag. He was a Boy Scout."

Kara was so happy.
Pam was happy, too.

"I am glad we found out about Brownie Scouts," said Mom. "It sounds like fun."

"We must go now," said Mom. "It has been about an hour, and I have to put my pie in the oven."

Kara gave a loud shout. "Yippee!" she said. "I am going to be a Brownie Scout!"

The End

The Snowman

By Hetty Hubbard

Illustrations by Ellen Joy Sasaki

Vocabulary Words

blow
1. blows

2. bow

3. crow

4. grow

5. growing

6. Owen

7. row

slow
8. slowly

9. show

10. snow

snow balls
11. snowballs

12. snowing

snow man
13. snowman

14. window

Story Words

15. Becky

but tons
16. buttons

17. carrot

18. Karen

19. stones

20. tie

21. winter

It was the first snow of
the winter. Owen, Karen,
and Becky ran out to
make a big snowman.

"The north wind blows, and we have snow and a snowman!" said Dad from the window.

"Come see the fine show," he said. "The snowman is slowly growing."

"Here are two black coals so the snowman can see," said Owen.

"Here is a carrot for a nose," said Becky.

"Let's add a bow tie at the neck," said Karen.

Dad said to Mom,
"Let's get a hat for the
snowman. We can go
out and help the children."

"OK," said Mom. Maybe
we can make some
snowballs. Out they went.

Mom put the hat on the snowman.

"Look, Dad! We put stones in a row for buttons," said Becky.

"Now, there is a snowman to crow about!" said Dad.

"If it keeps snowing, we may see it grow some more!" said Mom.

The End

The New Crew

By Lynda MacDonald and Sue Dickson

Illustrations by Lane Yerkes

Vocabulary Words

1. blew
2. crew
3. Drew
4. few
5. flew
6. mew
7. Newton
8. Stewart

Story Words

9. dragged
10. Drew's

11. even
12. hammers
13. happened
14. logs
15. making
16. mast
17. nails
18. rubbed
19. Stewart's
20. tools

"Let's make a raft to sail on the pond," said Stewart.

"OK," said Drew. "We can get a few logs at my house."

"I will get some tools and nails," said Stewart.

"Let's meet back at the pond," said Drew.

"OK," said Stewart.

On his way to the pond, Drew met Newton, his big cat. Newton rubbed Drew's leg.

"Do you want to help us?" asked Drew.

"Mew, mew," went Newton.

Drew and Stewart began
making the raft. The
hammers and nails flew!

At last, the raft was
finished. It even had a
sail on the mast!

Just as Stewart and Drew dragged the new raft into the pond, a bird flew to sit on the mast!

All at once, lots of things happened! Newton jumped onto the raft. As the cat jumped, a big puff of wind blew on the sail!

The rope flew out of Stewart's hand. Away went the raft!

"Look at the new crew!" yelled Drew.

Drew and Stewart both giggled at such a funny thing!

The End

Quite a Surprise

By Hetty Hubbard
Illustrations by Grace Lin

Vocabulary Words

1. queen
2. question
3. quiet
4. quilt
5. quit
6. quite
7. quiz

her self
11. herself

12. Mother's

13. Nadia

14. scraps

sur prise
15. surprise

Story Words

al ways
8. always

9. cloth

10. days

48

Nadia was so quiet these days. Mom asked her a question.

"What are you doing, Nadia? What are those little scraps of cloth?" she asked.

Nadia had hoped to surprise her Mom.

"I am making something for you," said Nadia. She hoped that Mom would not quiz her more.

When Nadia could hear her mom's quick steps come near, she would quit making the quilt.

"I must get this quilt finished on time," said Nadia to herself.

On Mother's Day,
Nadia's surprise was
finished.

"A quilt!" Mom cried
when she saw it. "It is
so pretty! This is quite
a surprise. Even a queen
would love this quilt,
Nadia!"

Mom gave Nadia a big hug. "Thank you, Nadia," she said. "I will always see your love in each little stitch of that quilt! Thank you for a very happy Mother's Day!"

The End

The New White Car

By Hetty Hubbard

Illustrations by Mary Bono

Vocabulary Words

1. awhile
2. wheat
3. Wheelers
4. where
5. which
6. whipping
7. Whisk

Story Words

8. Abby
9. brëød
10. else

11. rolls
12. sandwiches
13. shall
14. sīgn
15. sīgns

The Wheelers have a new white car. They are going on a day trip in it.

Dad will take the wheel
and drive for awhile. Mom
will look at the map to
see which roads to take.

Abby and Frank will
look at the road signs so
they can tell where they
are and when to turn.

"What is that growing over there?" asked Frank.
"That is wheat," said Dad.

Mom asked, "Who can tell me what is made from wheat?"

"Flour!" yelled Frank.

"Bread!" yelled Abby.

"What else?" asked Mom.
"Sandwich rolls," said
Dad. "Shall we stop at
the next sandwich place
we see?"

"Look at that sign," said
Abby. "I can read it:
W-h-i-s-k! Whisk Inn!"

"See their flag whipping
in the wind?" asked Mom.

"I see it," said Frank.
"Sandwiches. Ice Cream.
Let's whisk in there, Dad."

"It looks like a nice
place," said Mom. "Yes,
let's whisk in there."

"When we come back out, it will be Mom's turn to drive our new car," said Dad.

"Good!" said Mom. "That will be fun."

The End